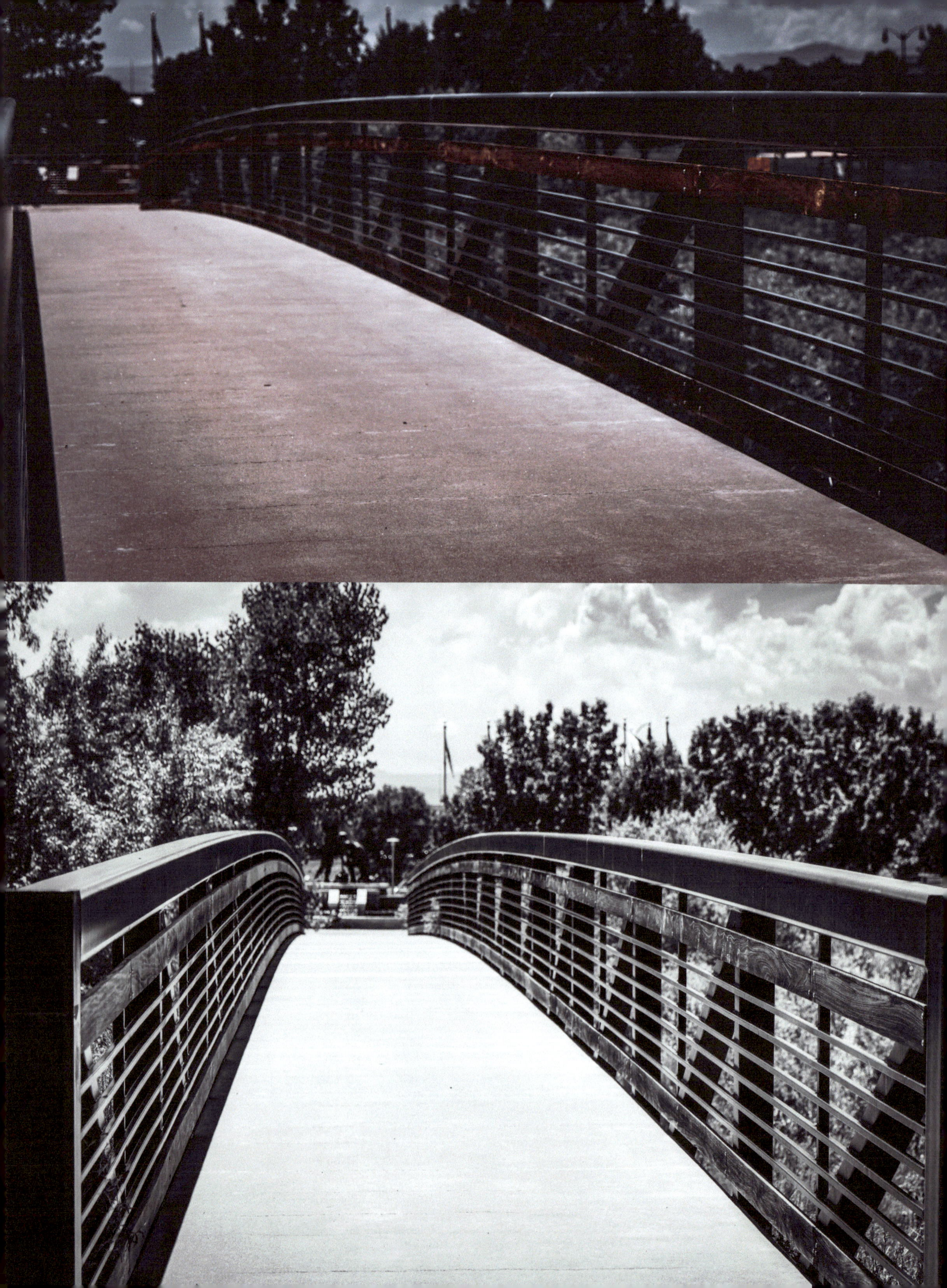

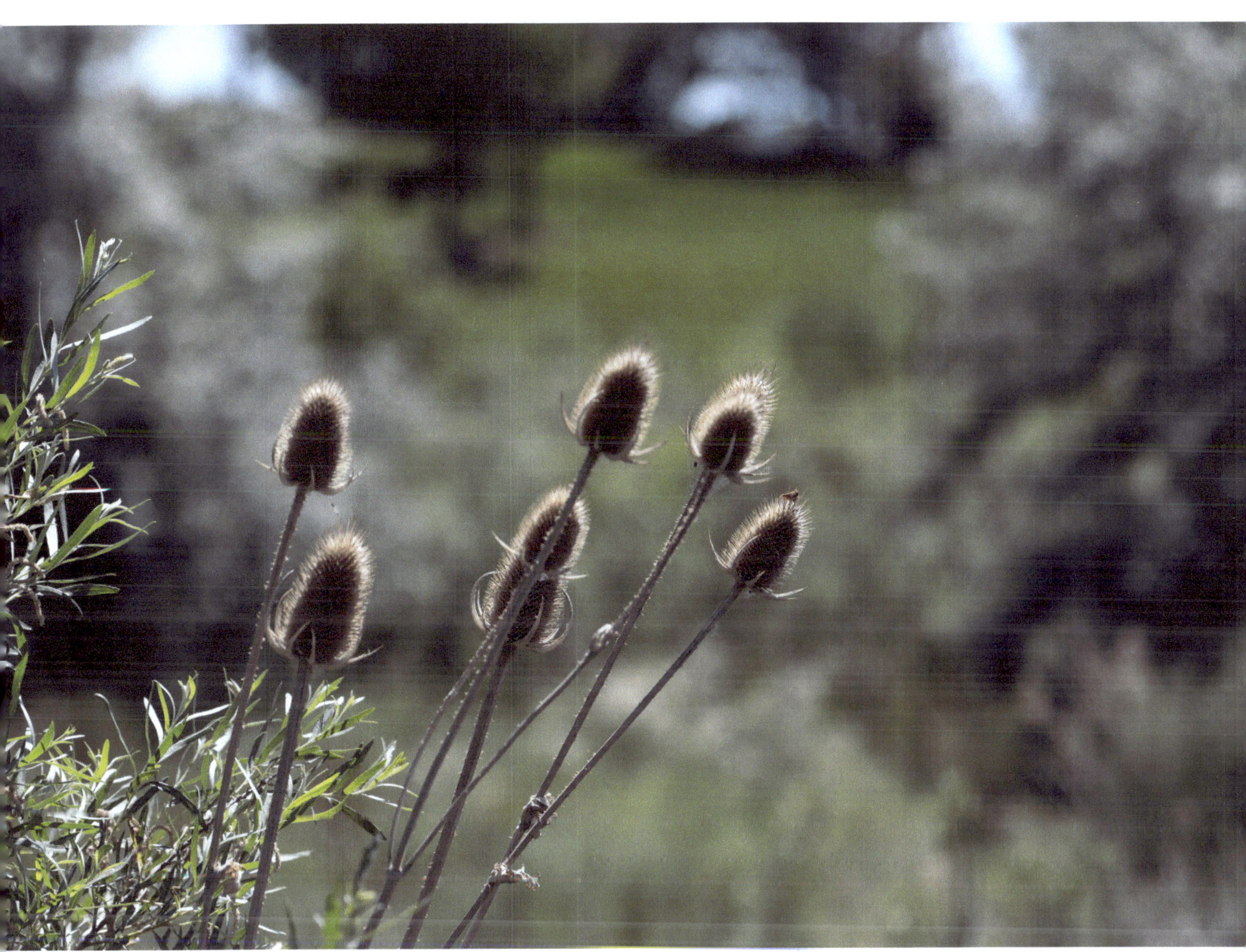

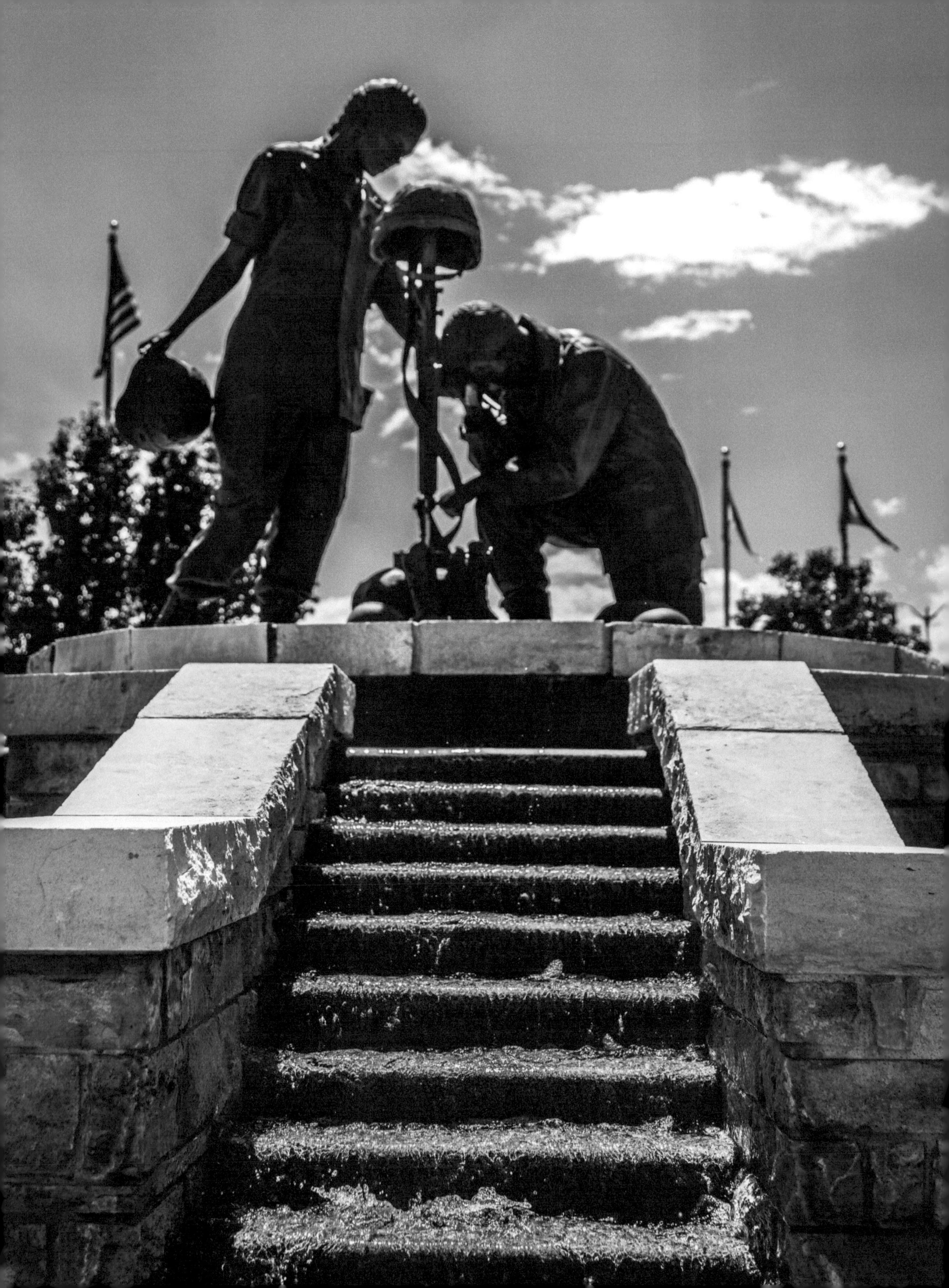

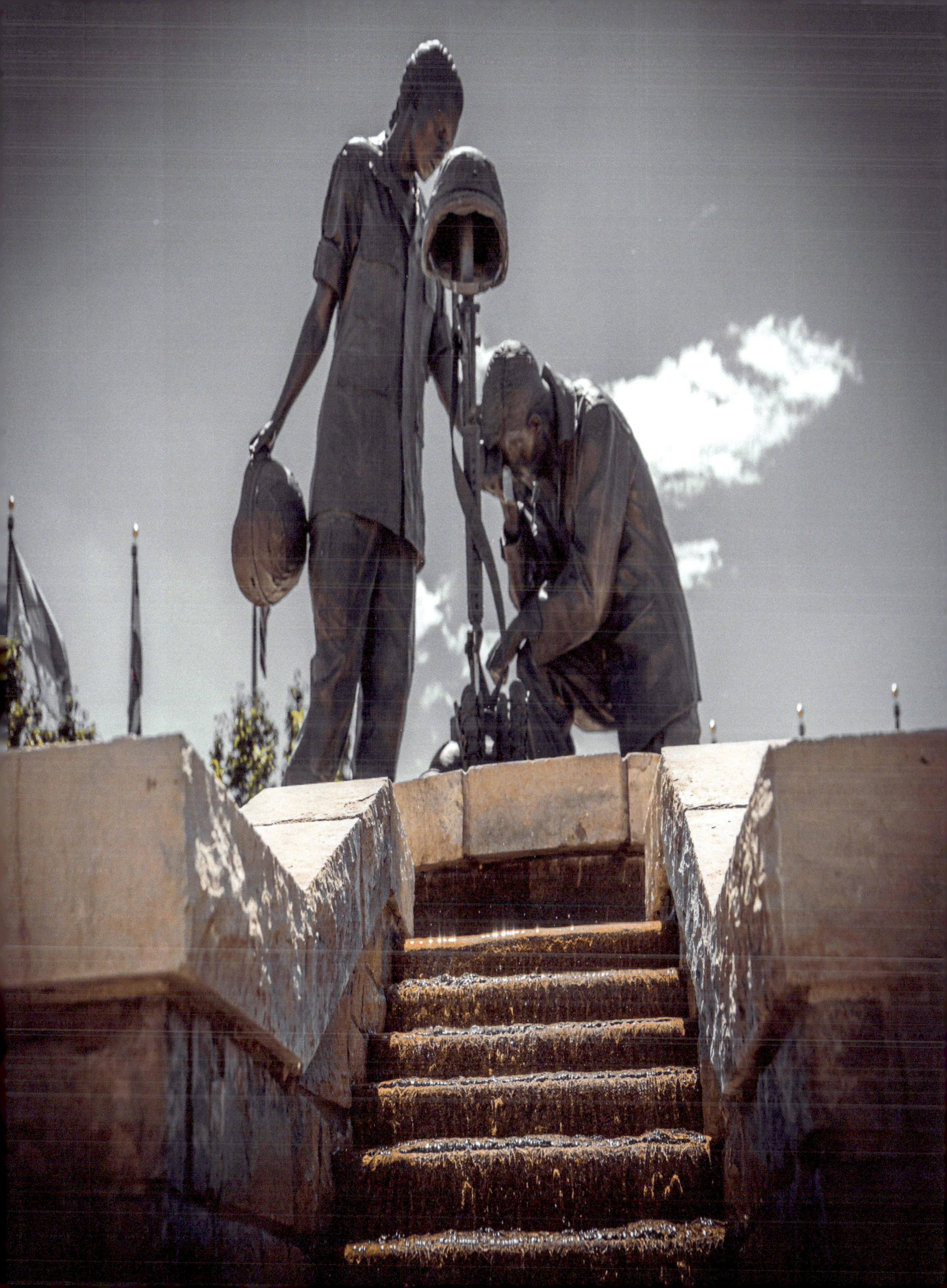

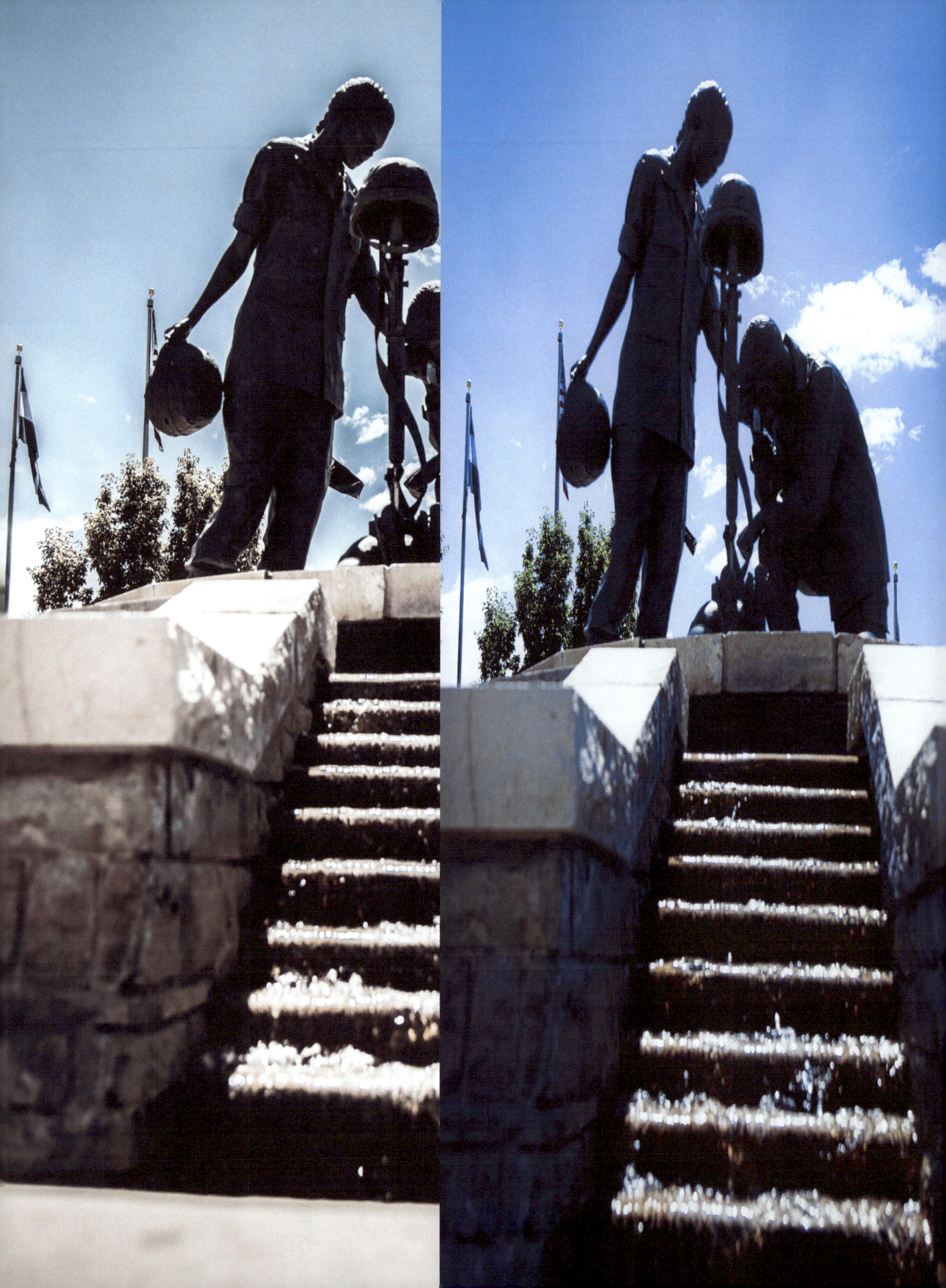

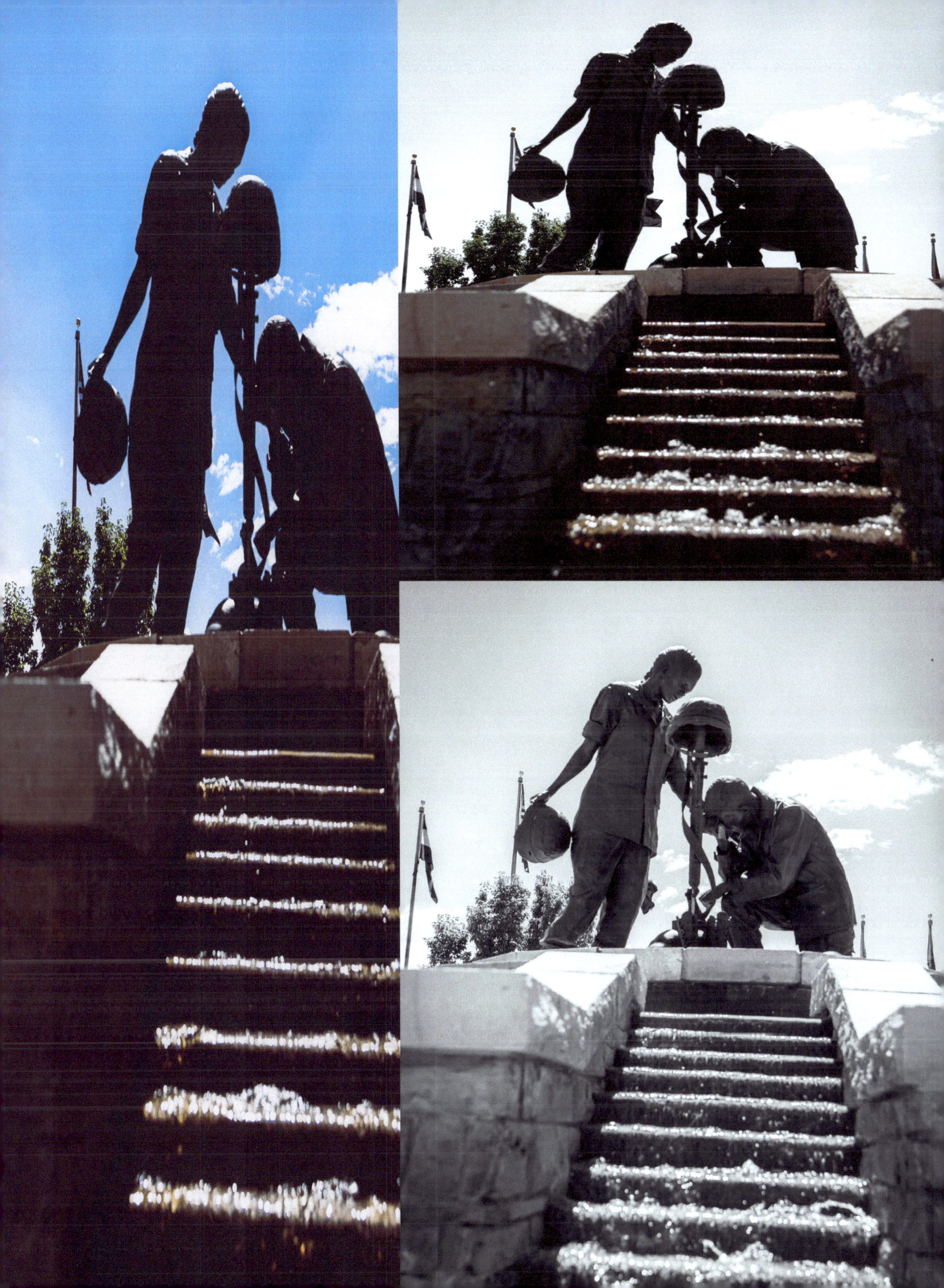

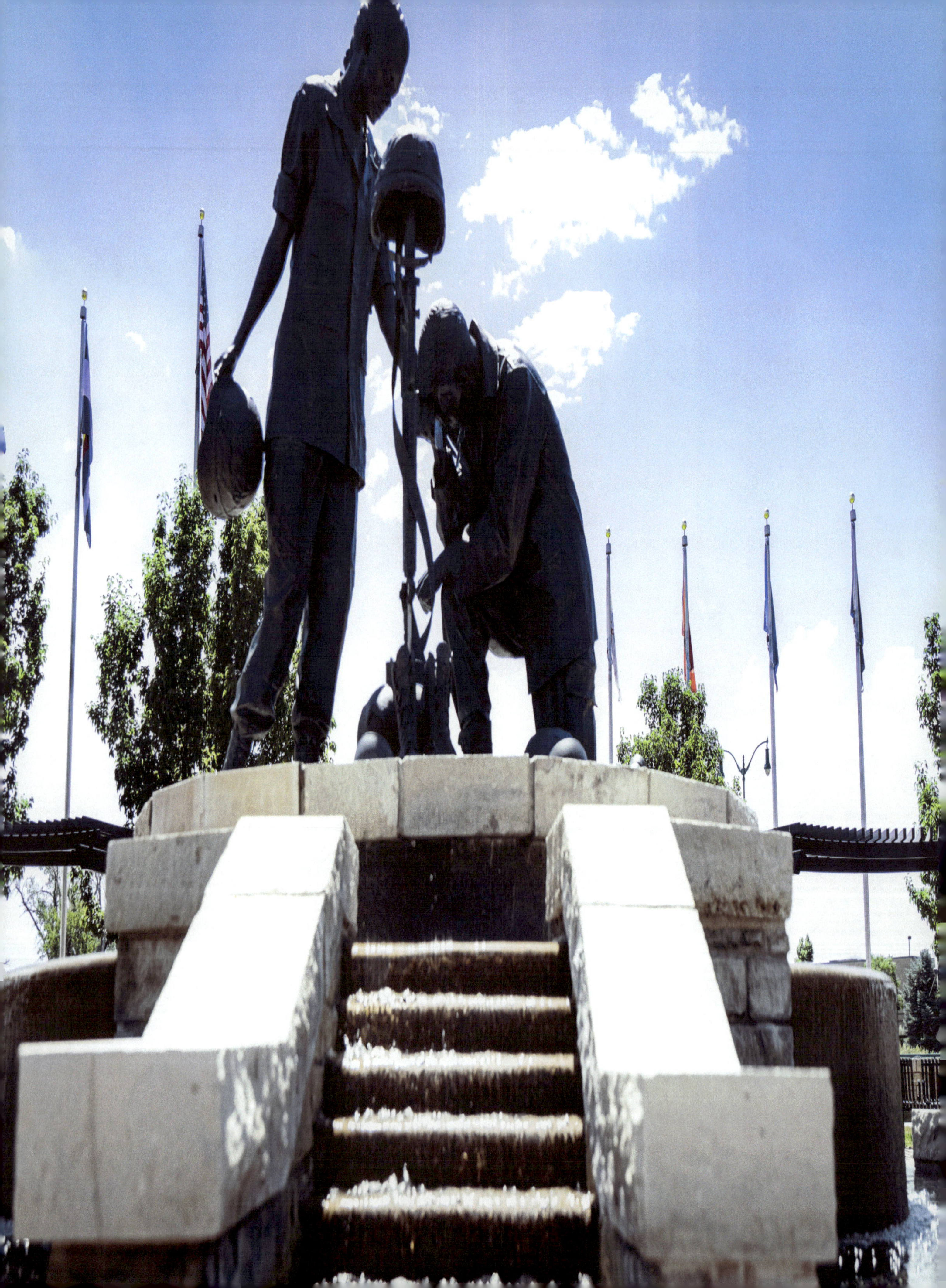

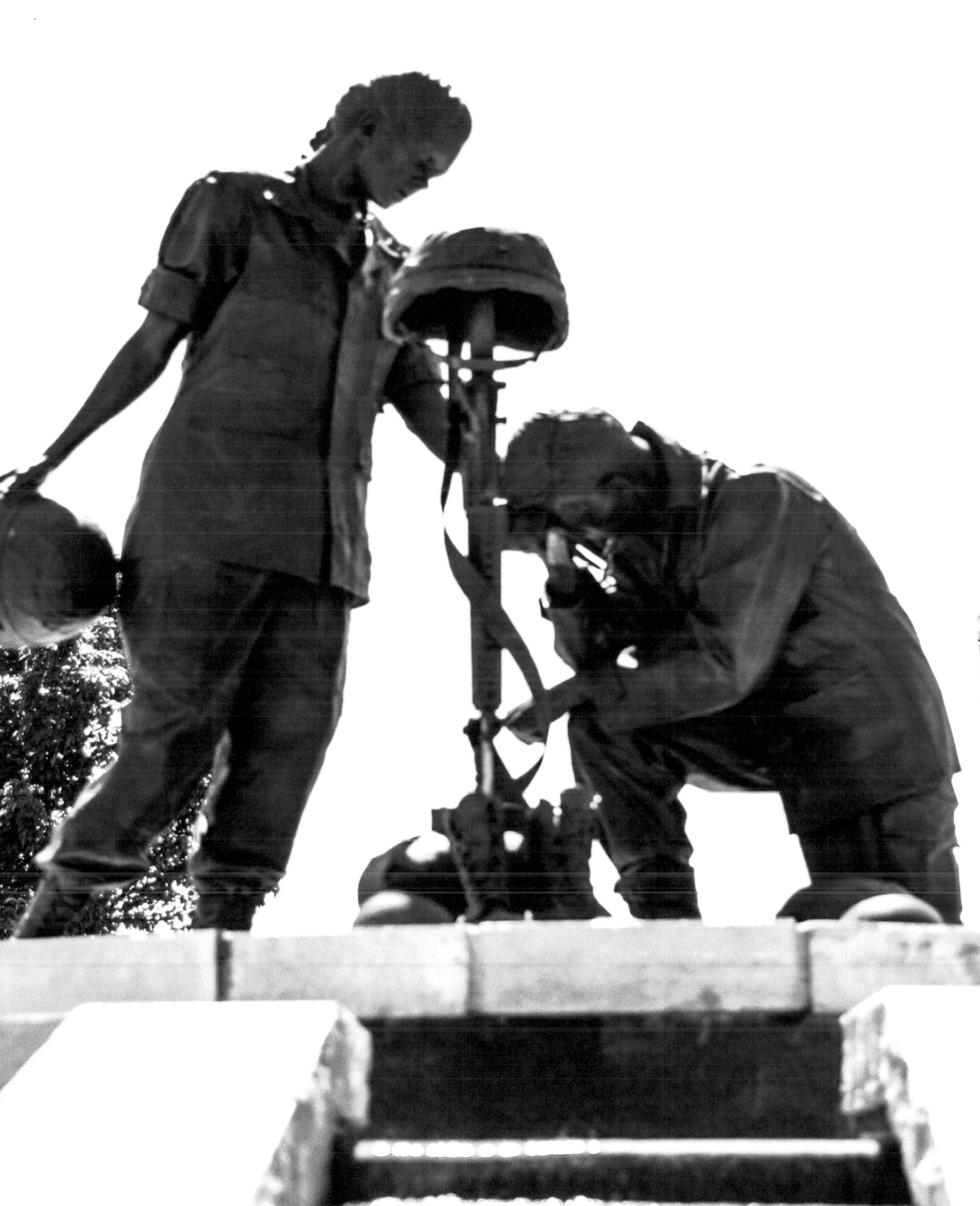

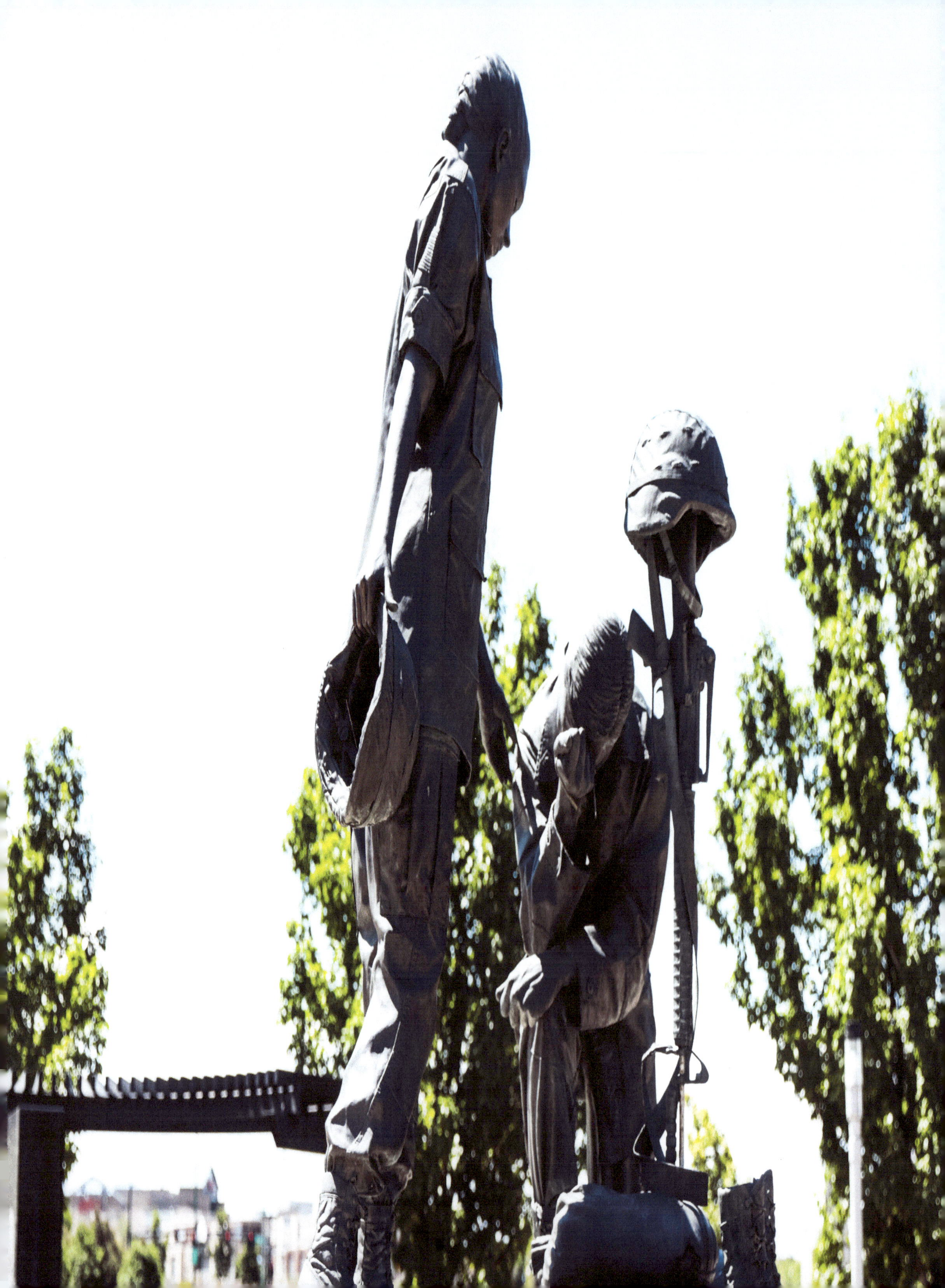

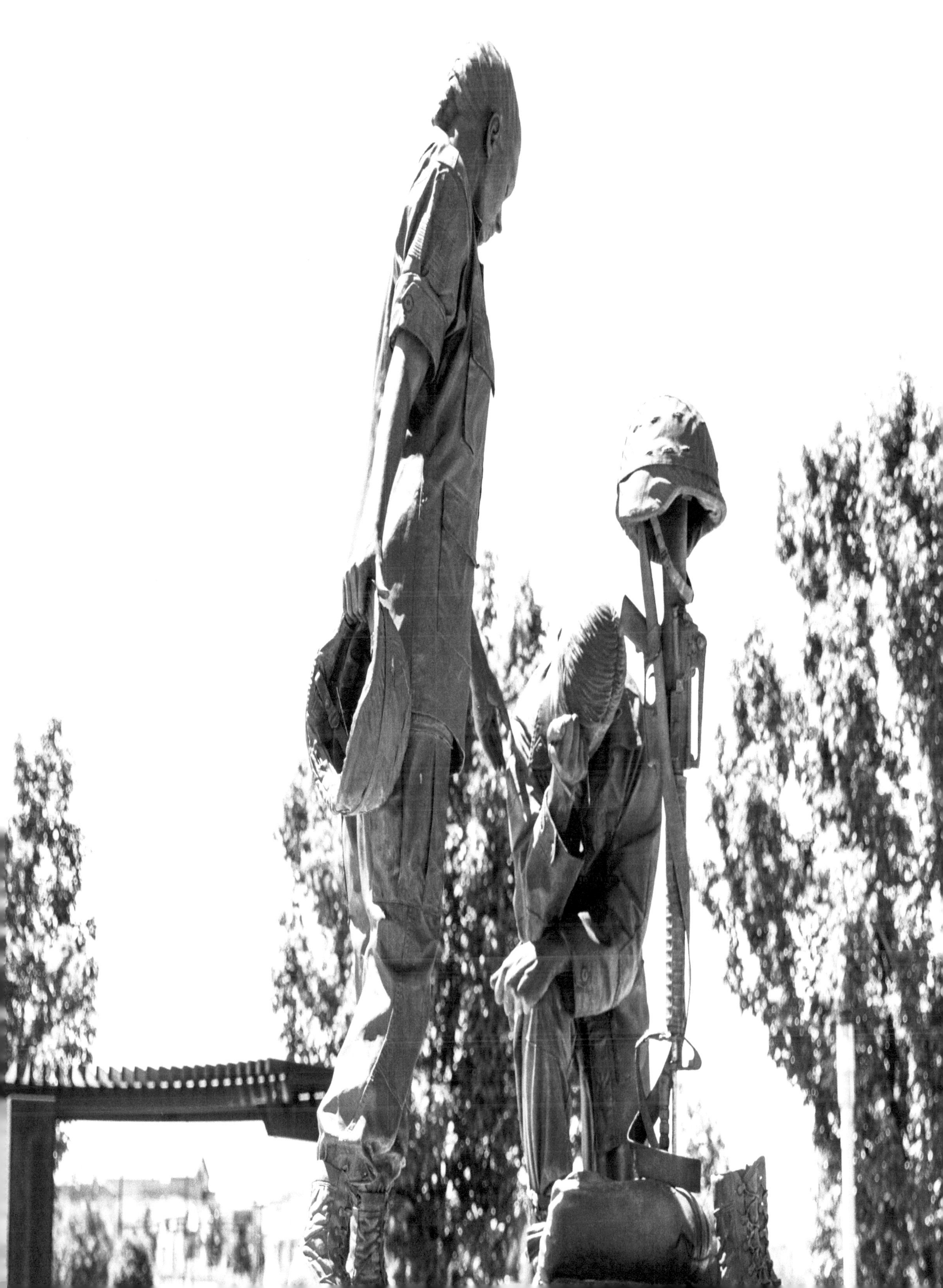

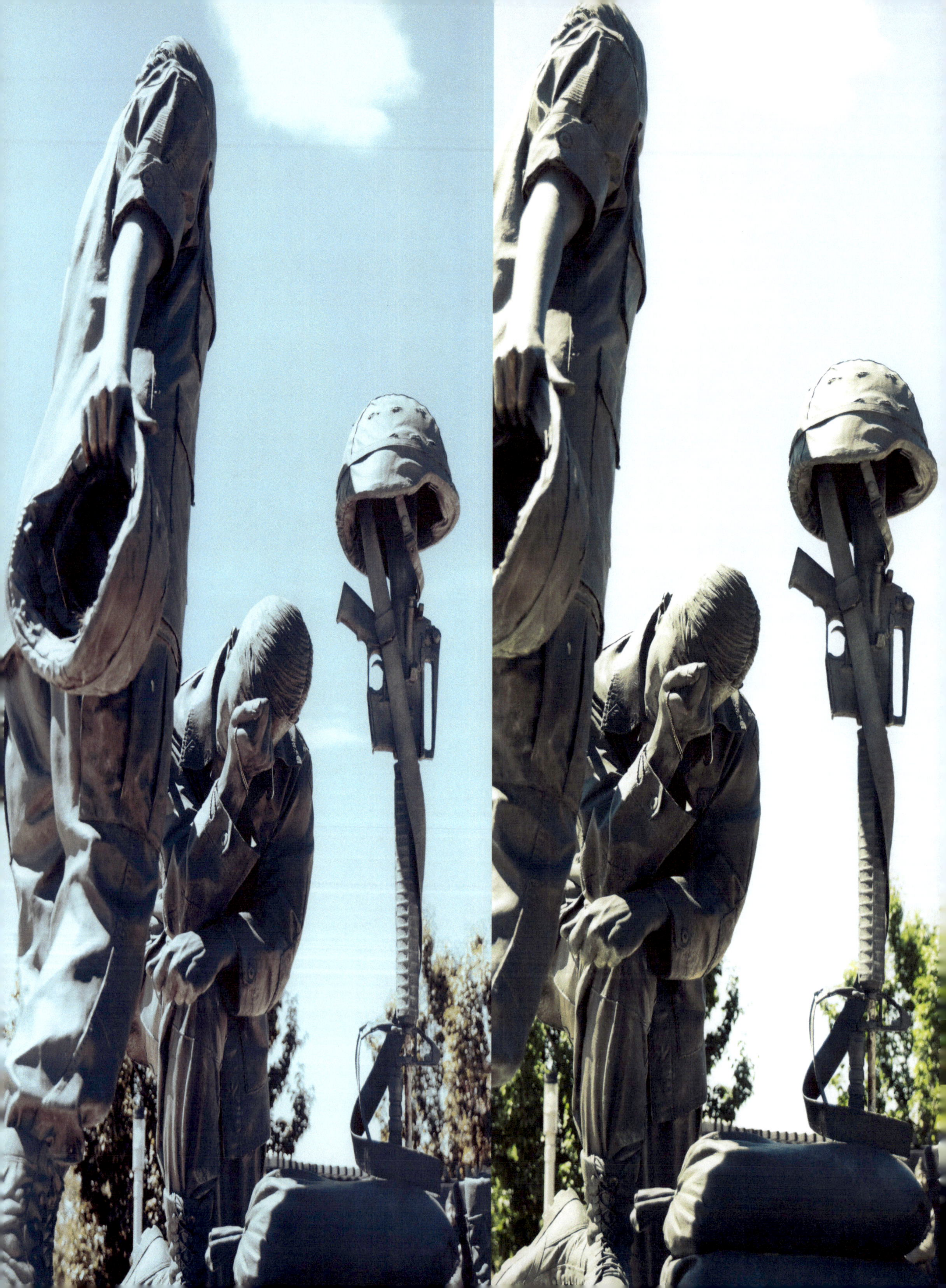

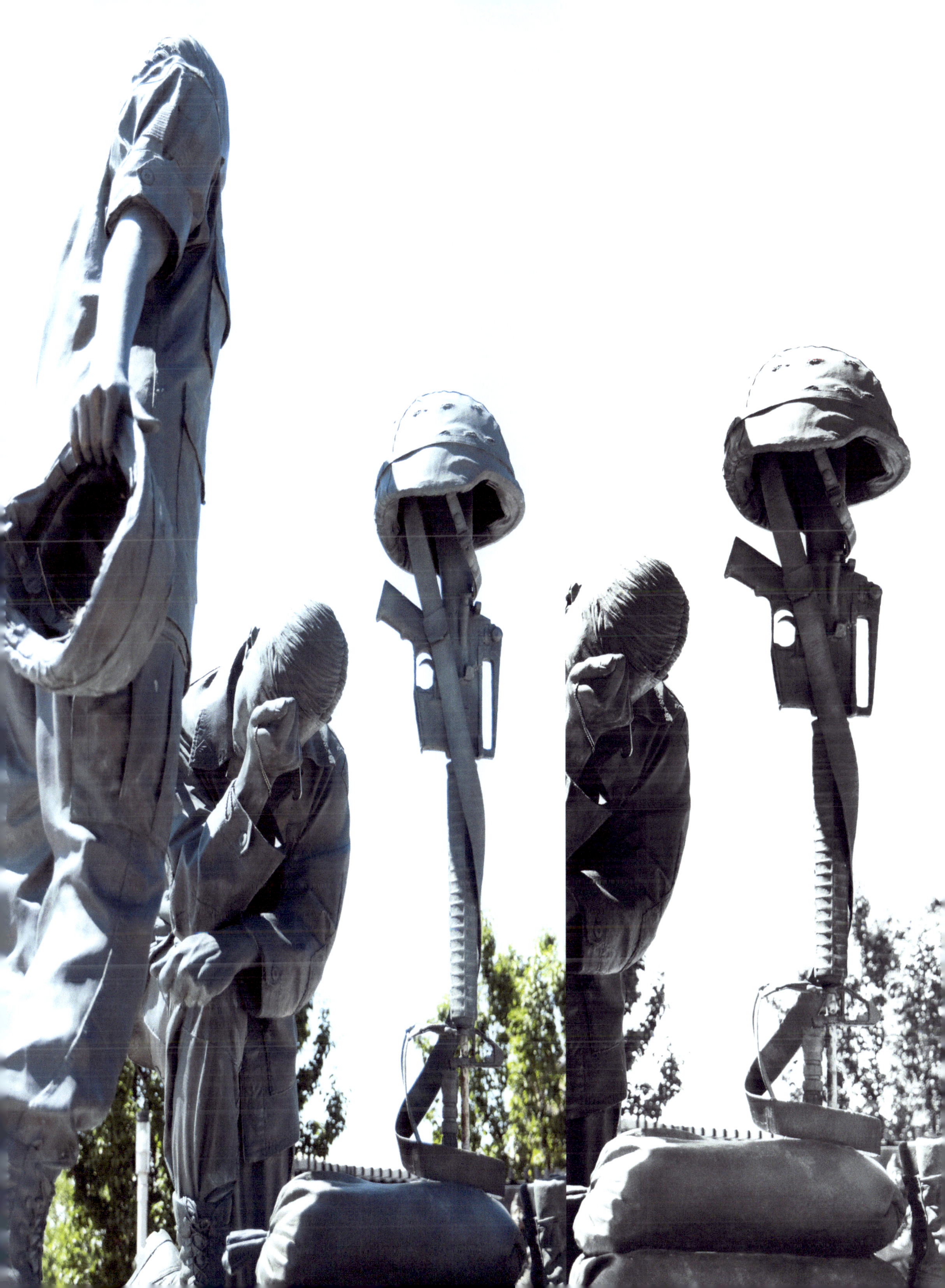

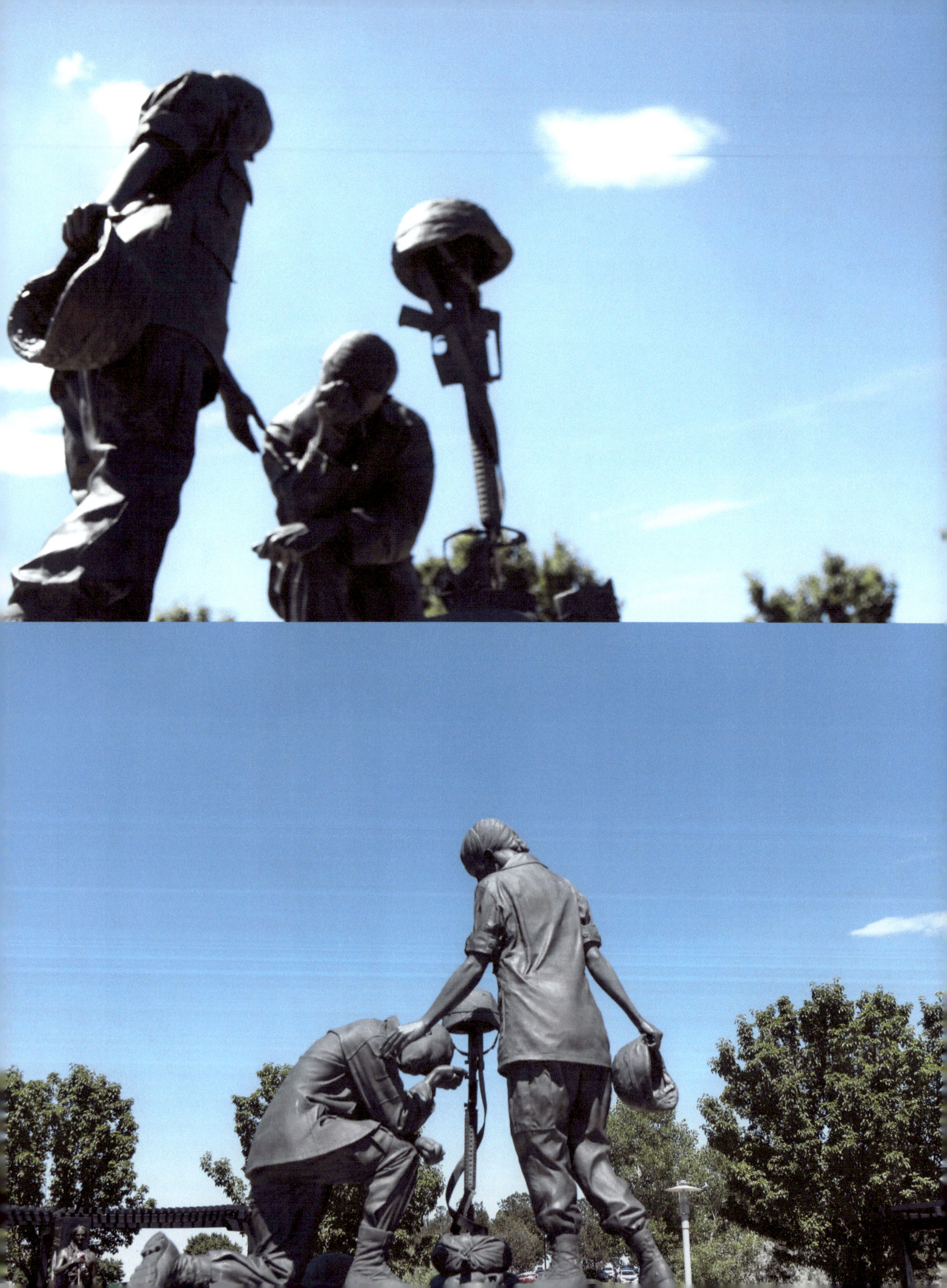

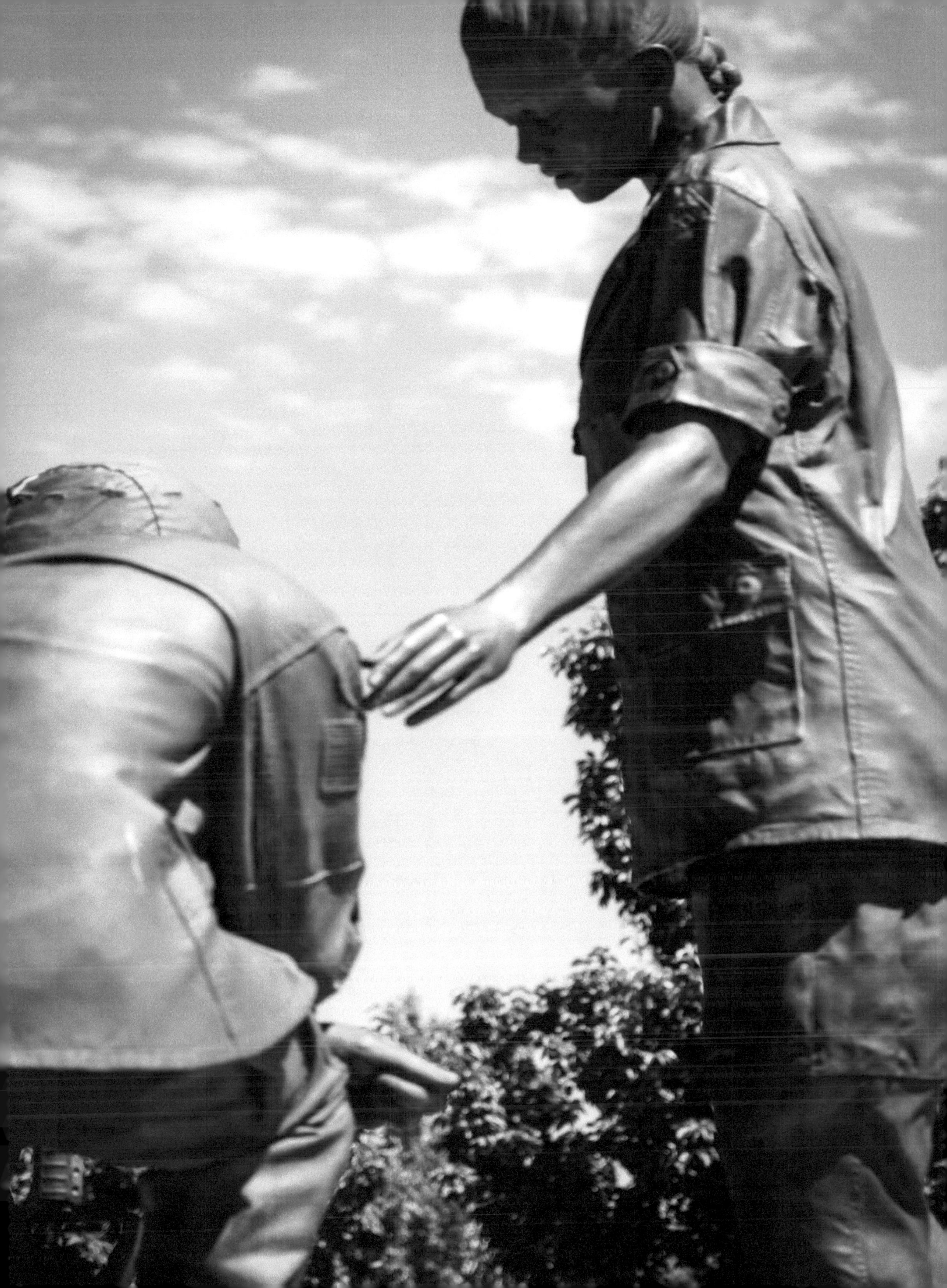

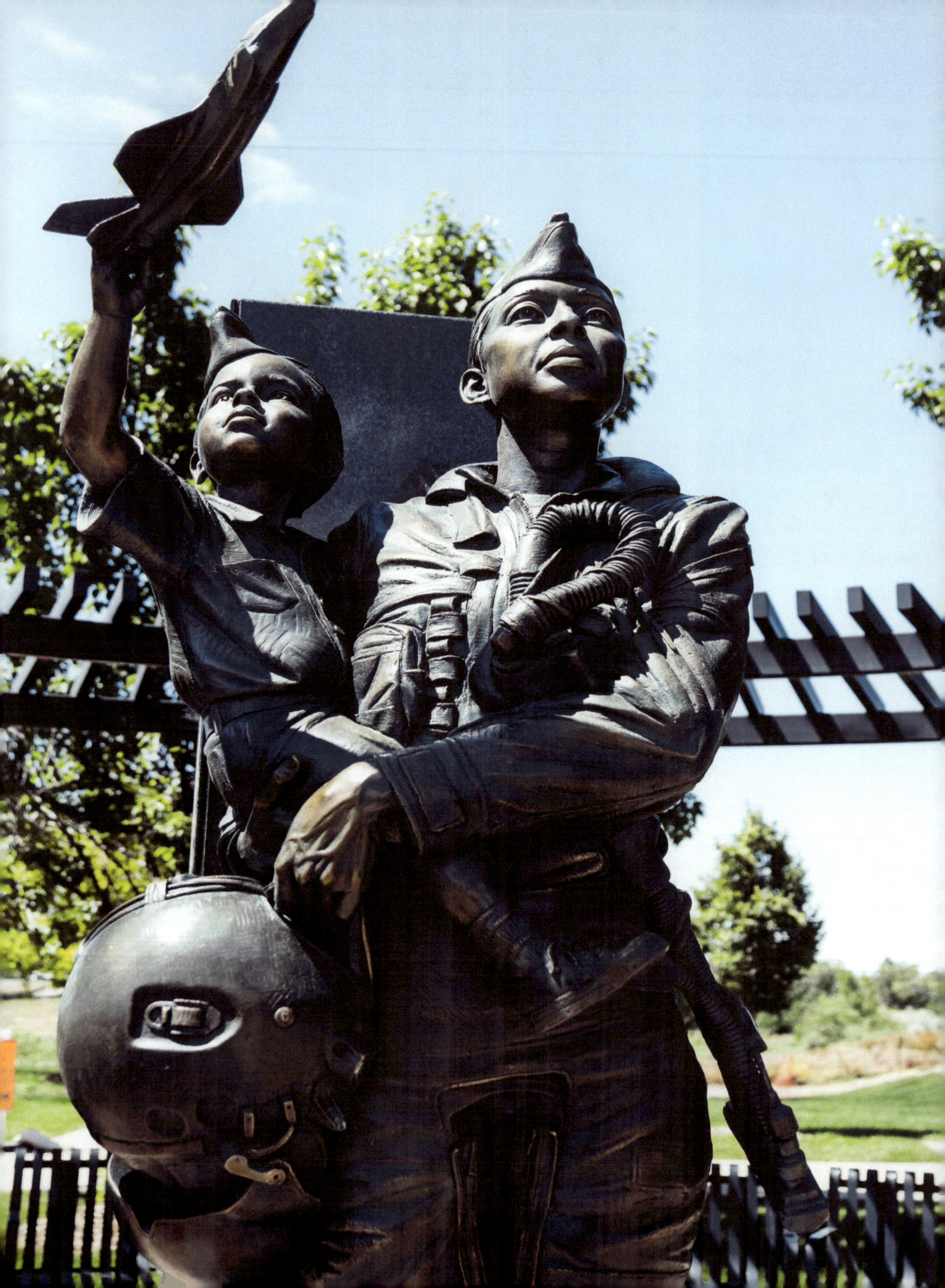

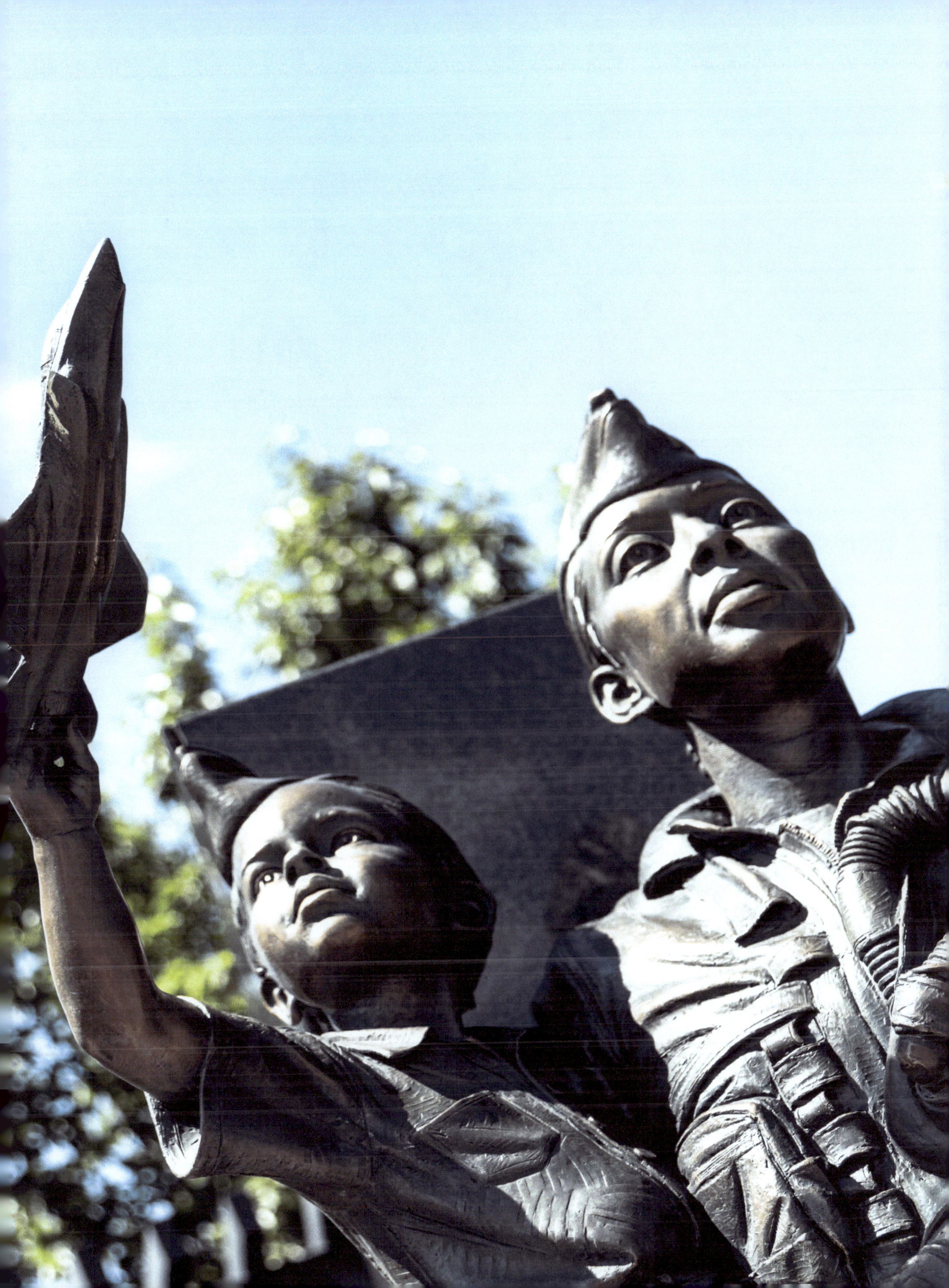

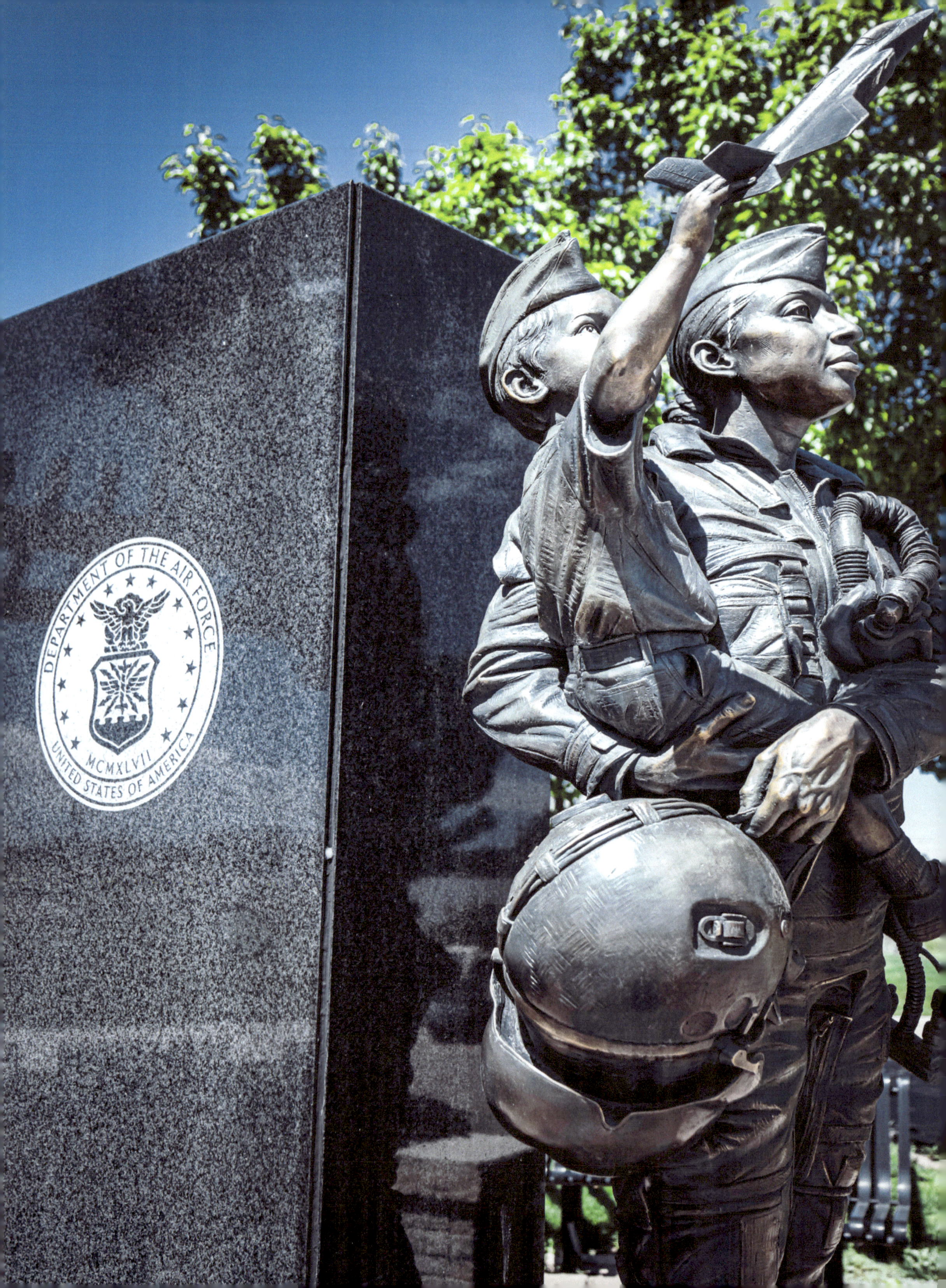

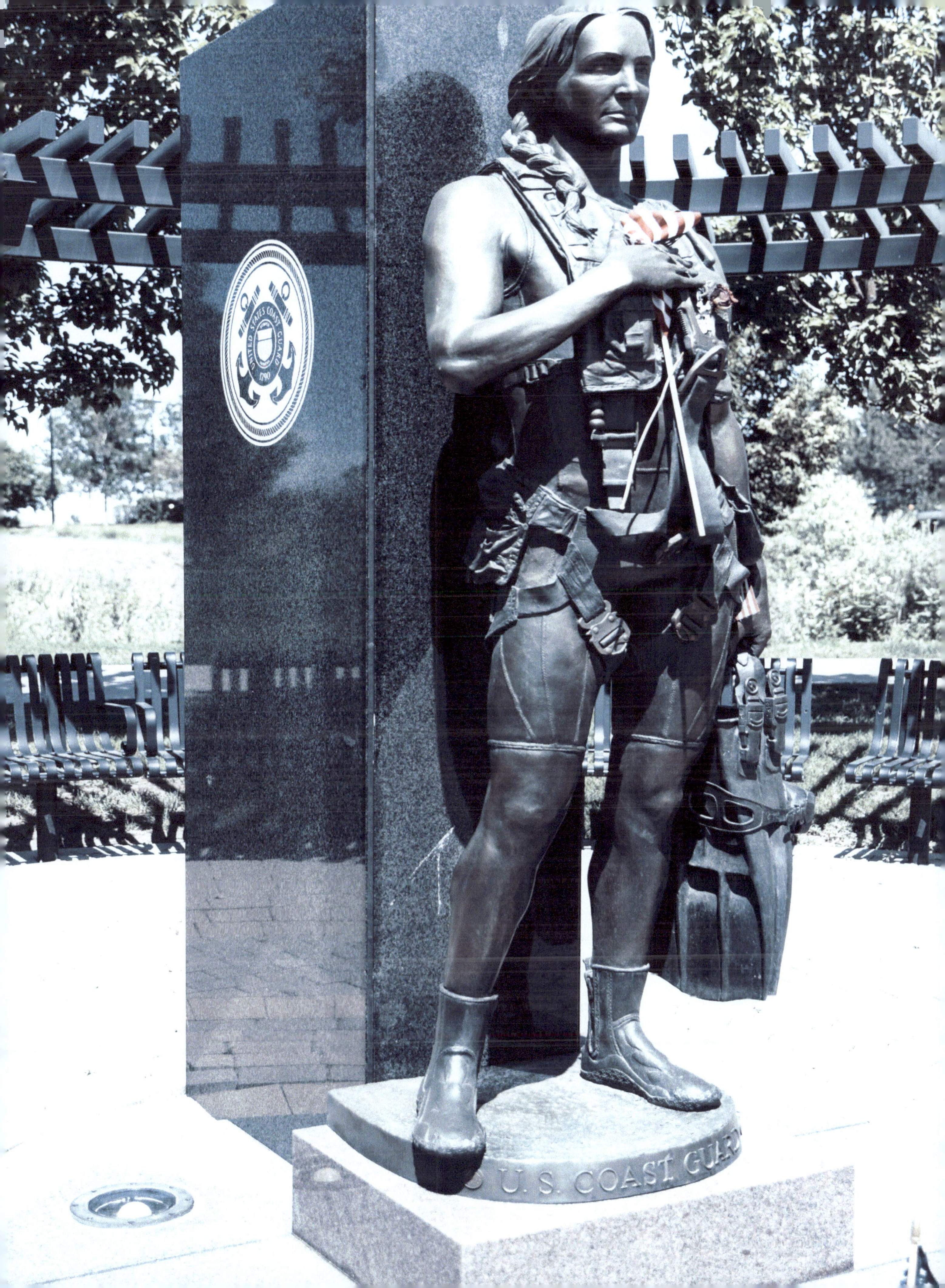

UNITED STATES COAST GUARD
1790
U. S. COAST GUARD

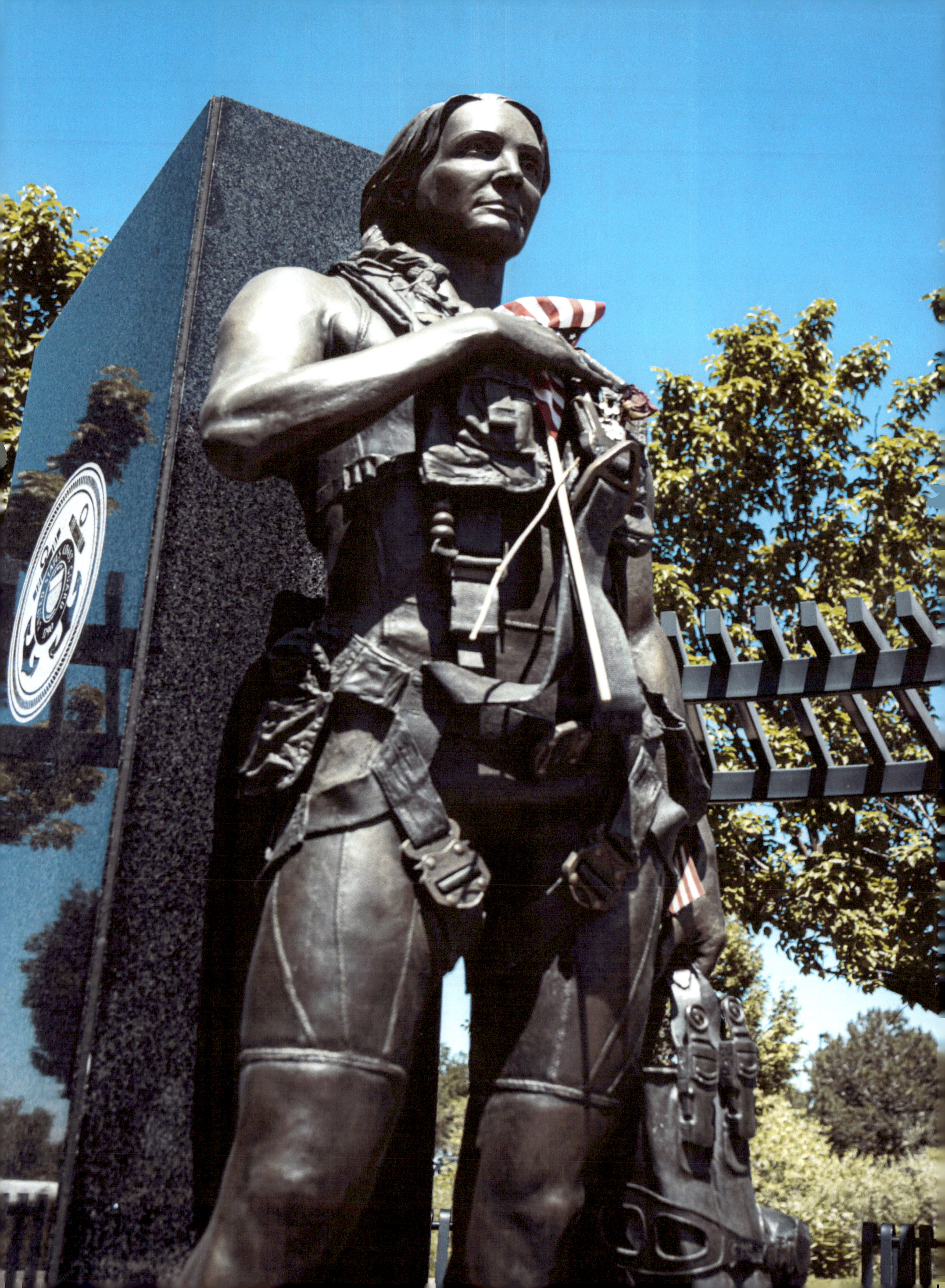

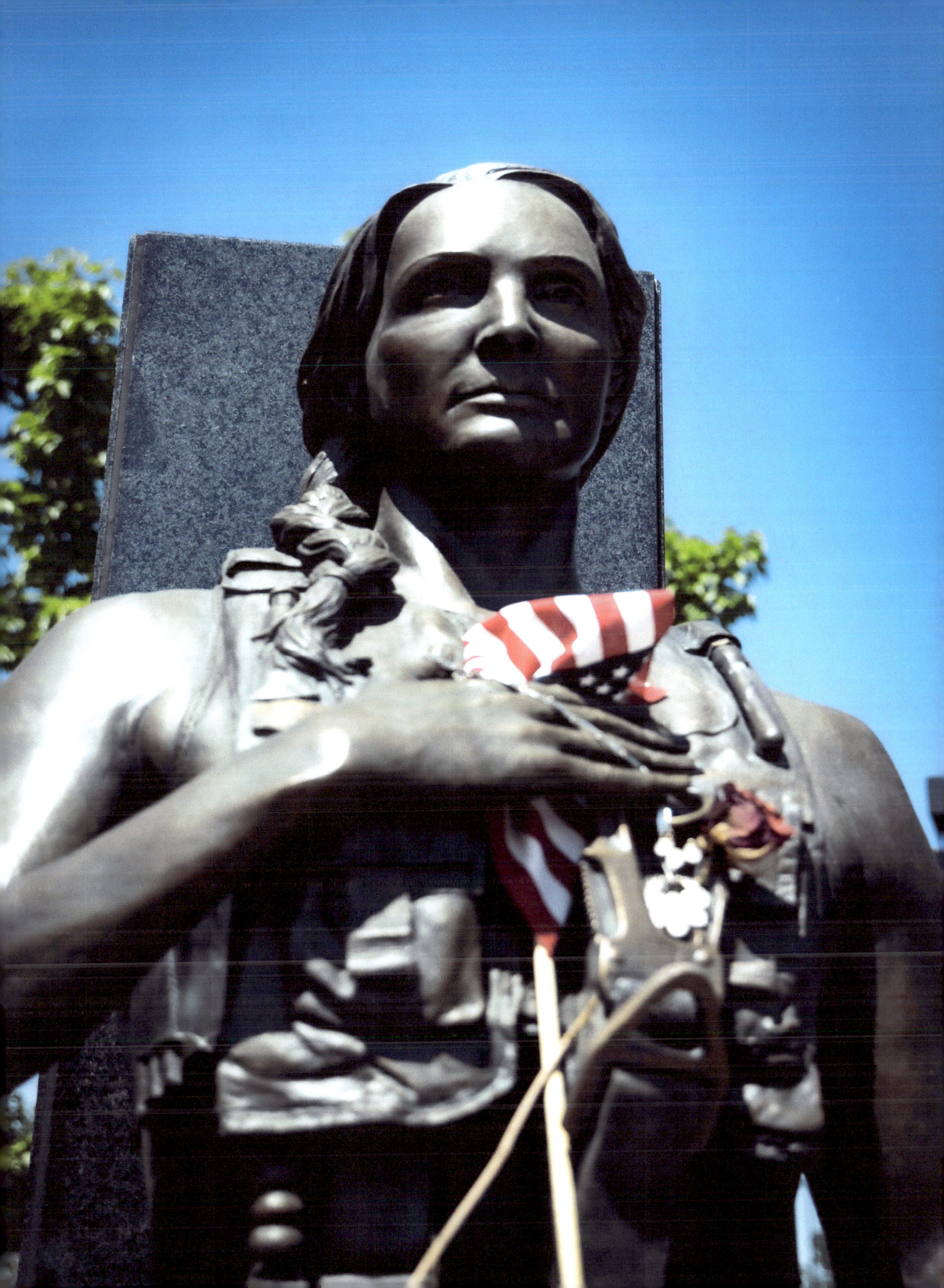

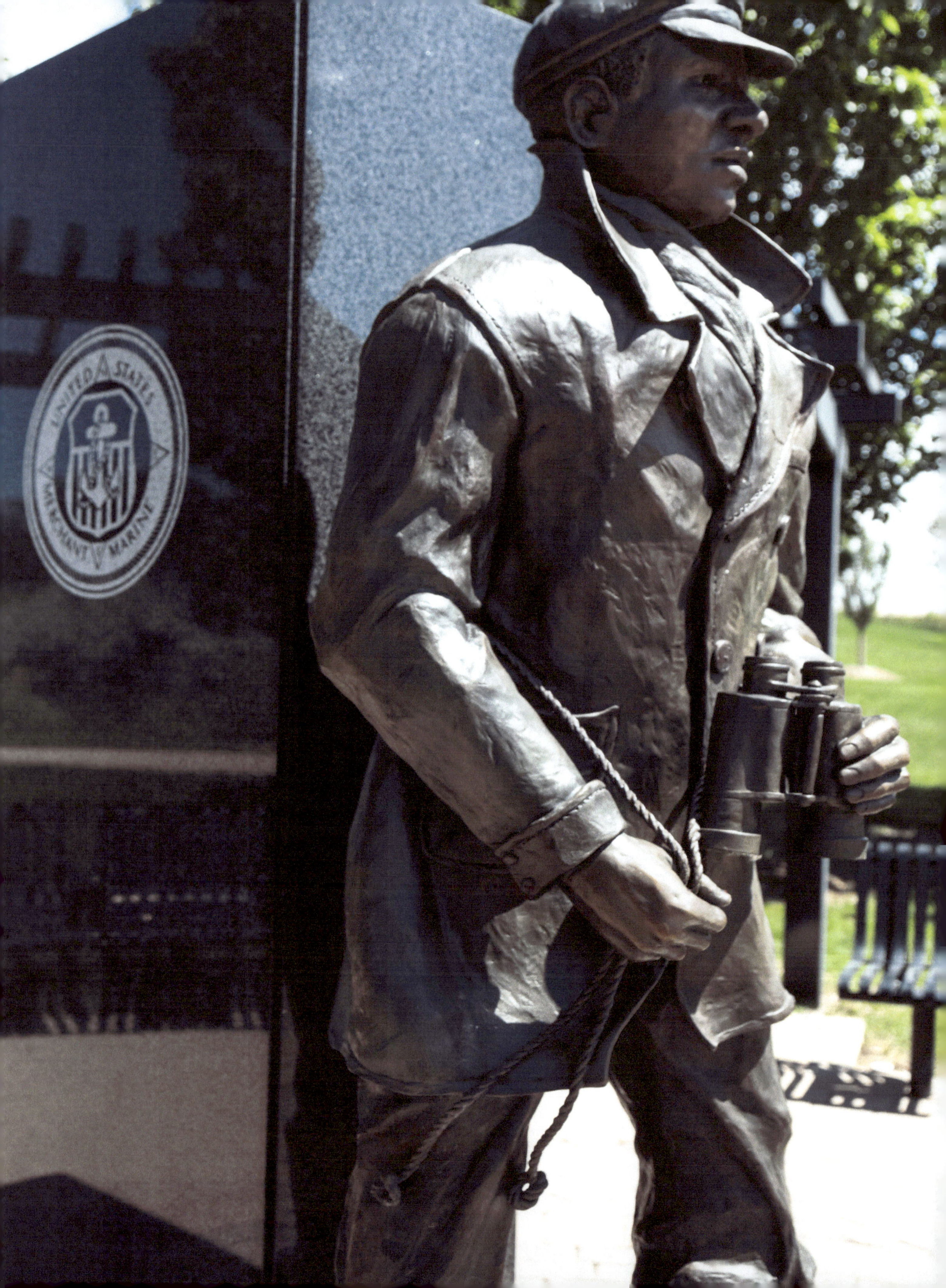

UNITED STATES
MERCHANT MARINE

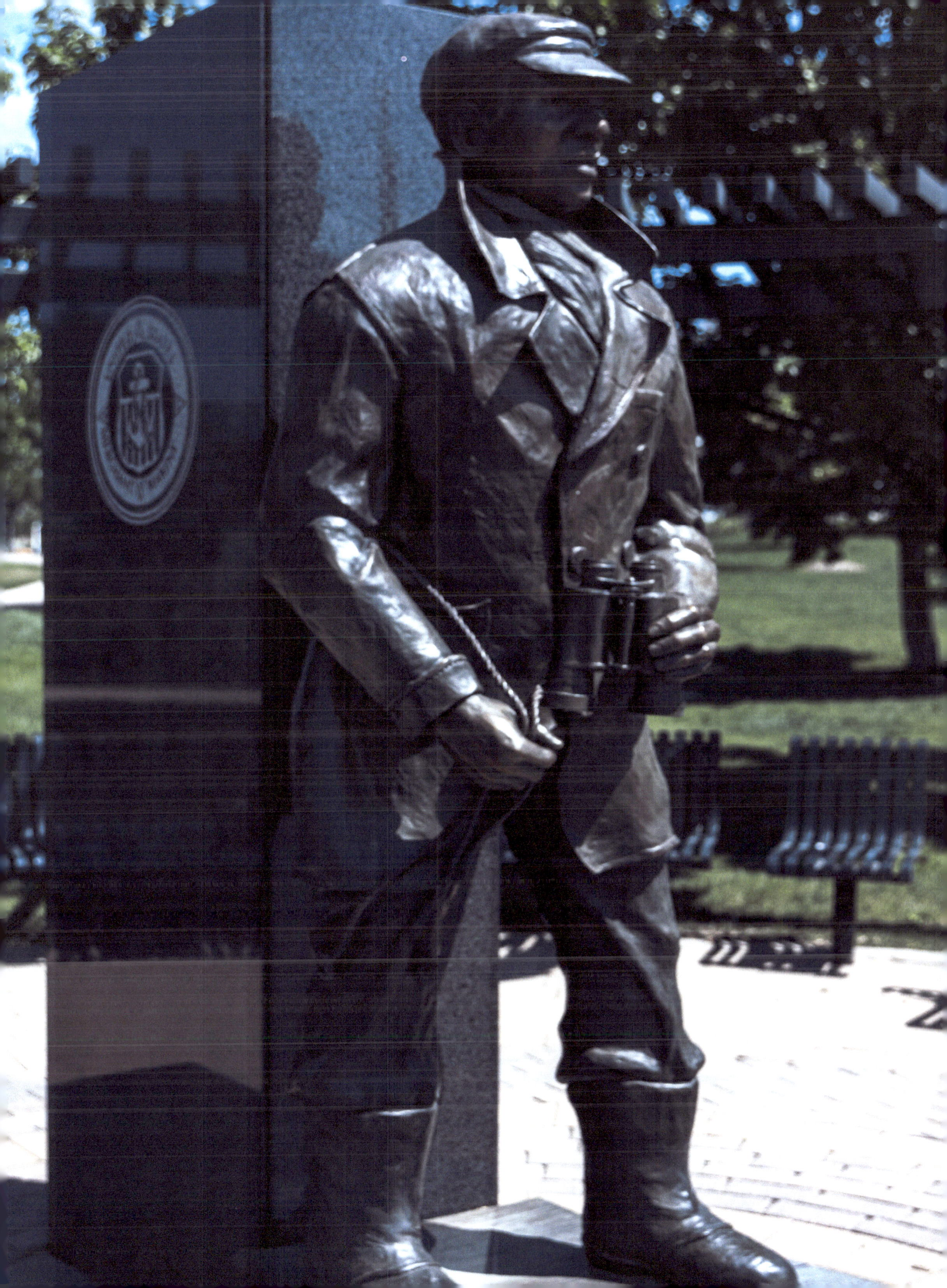

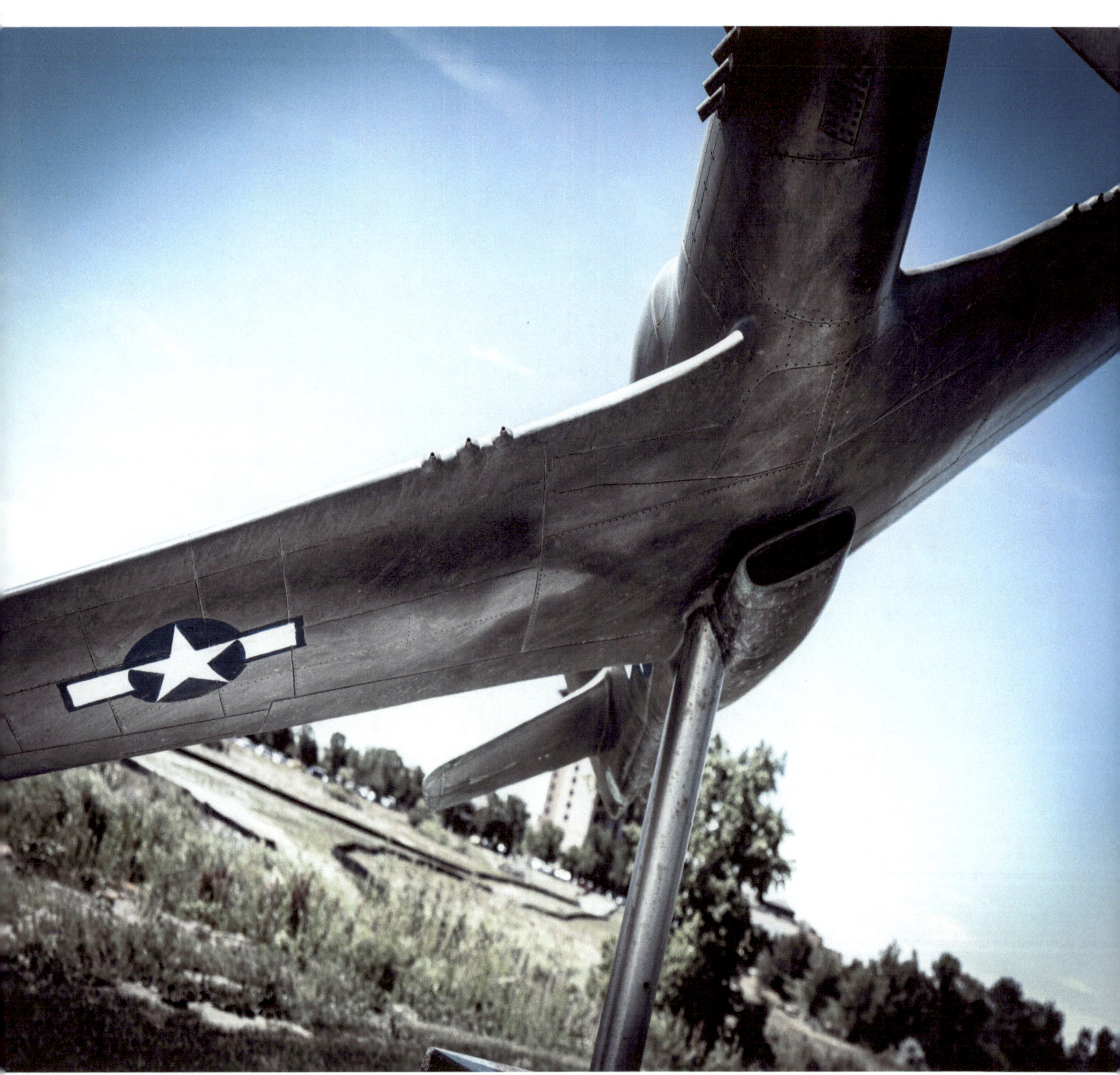

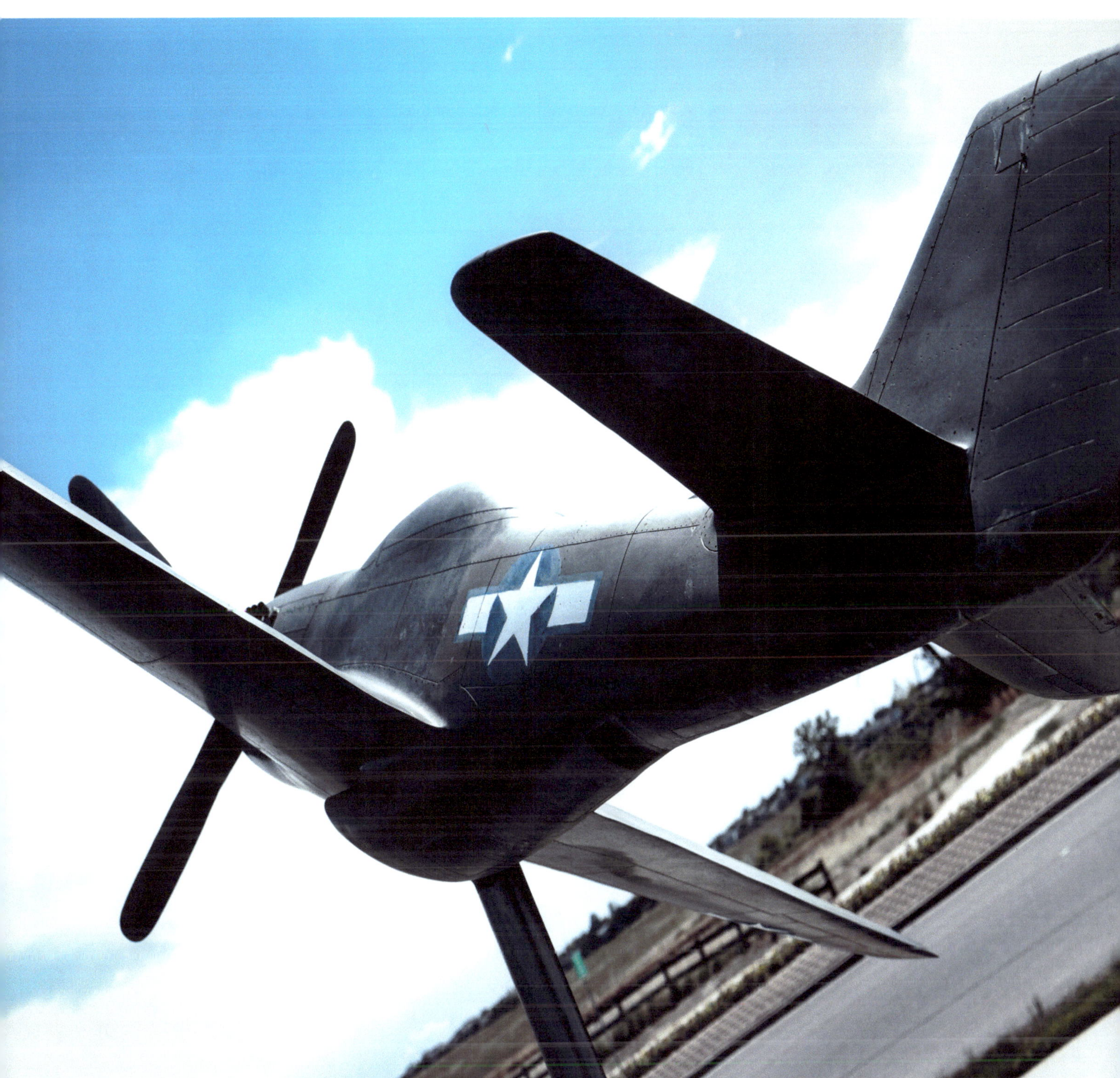

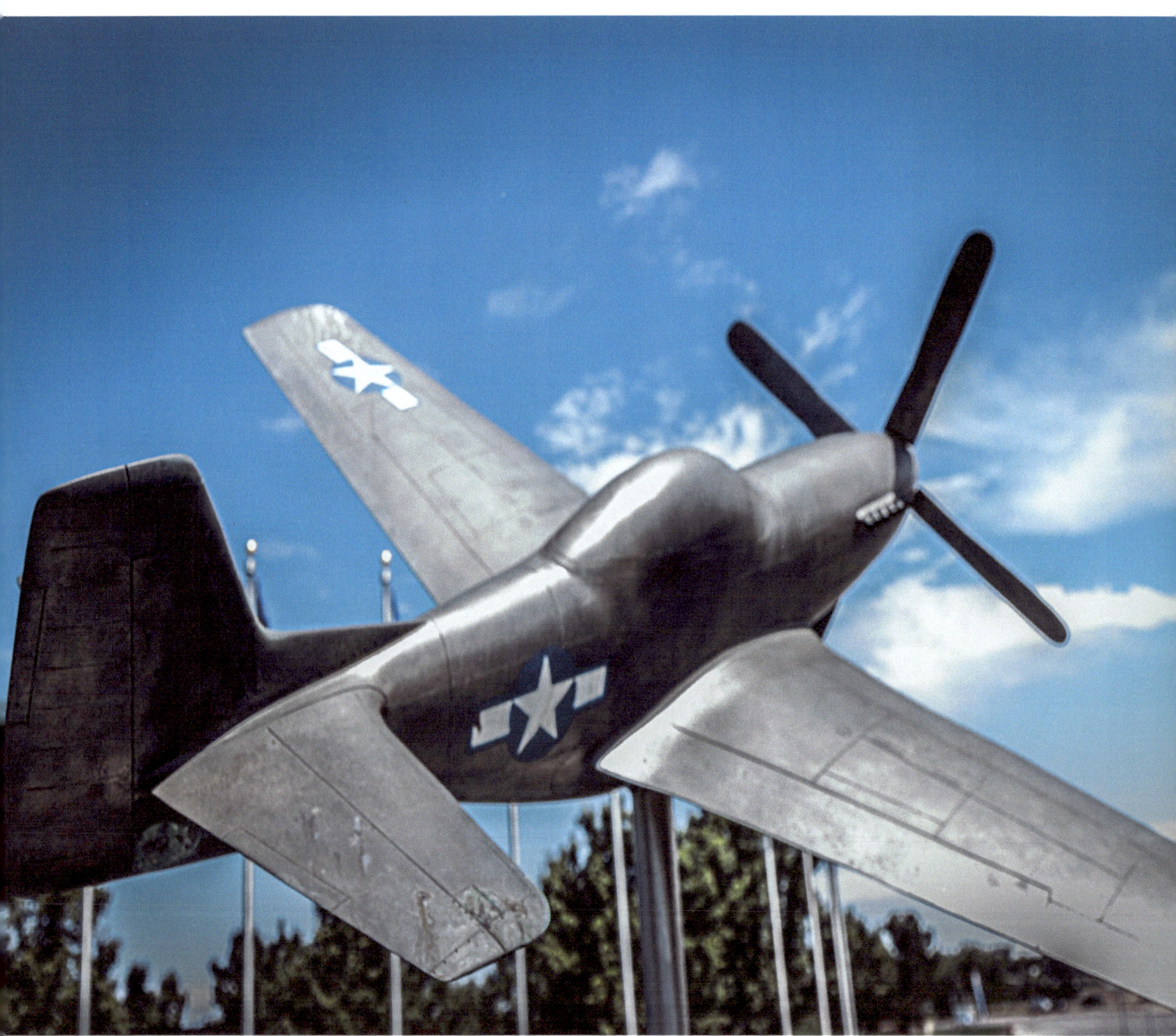

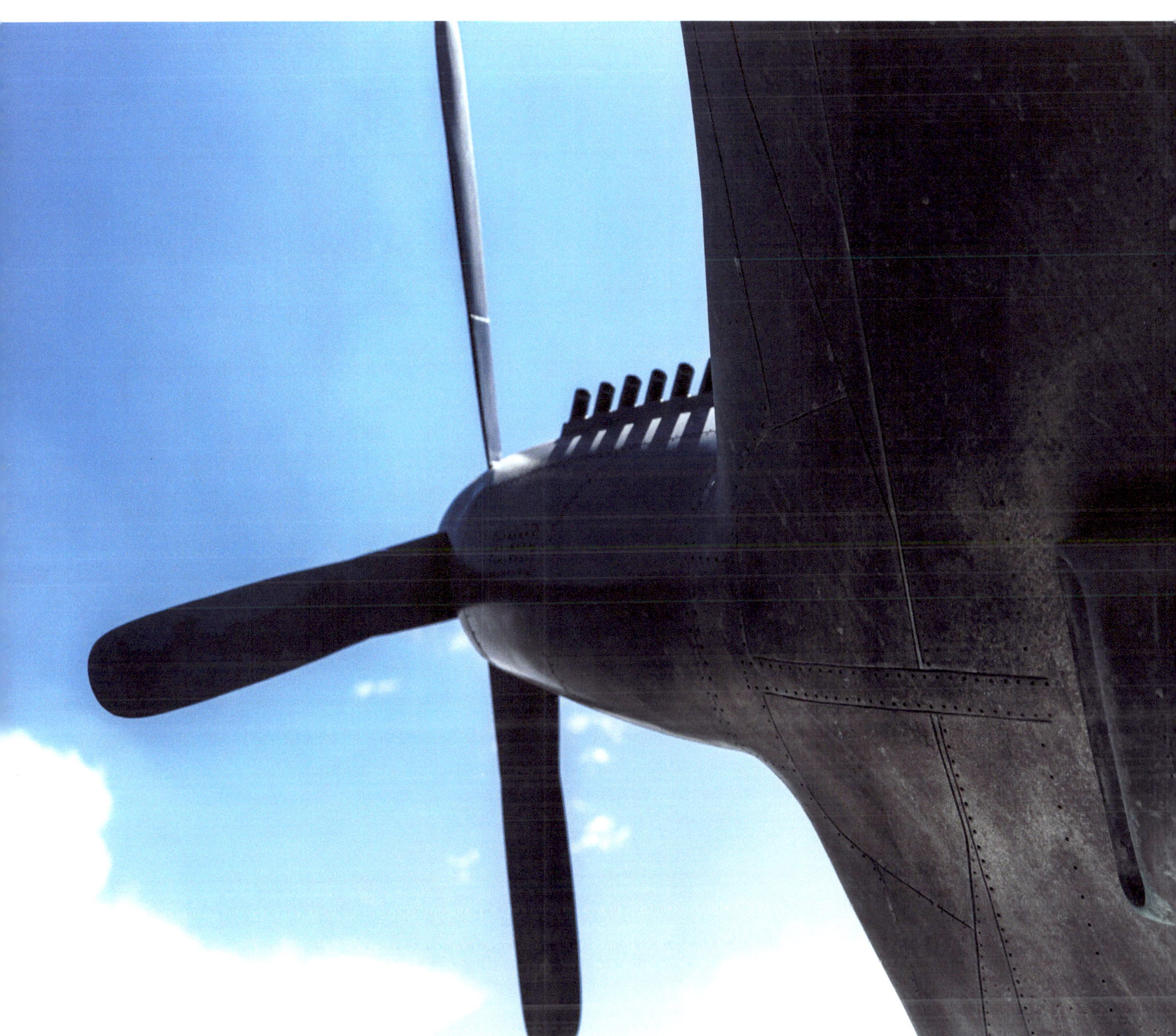

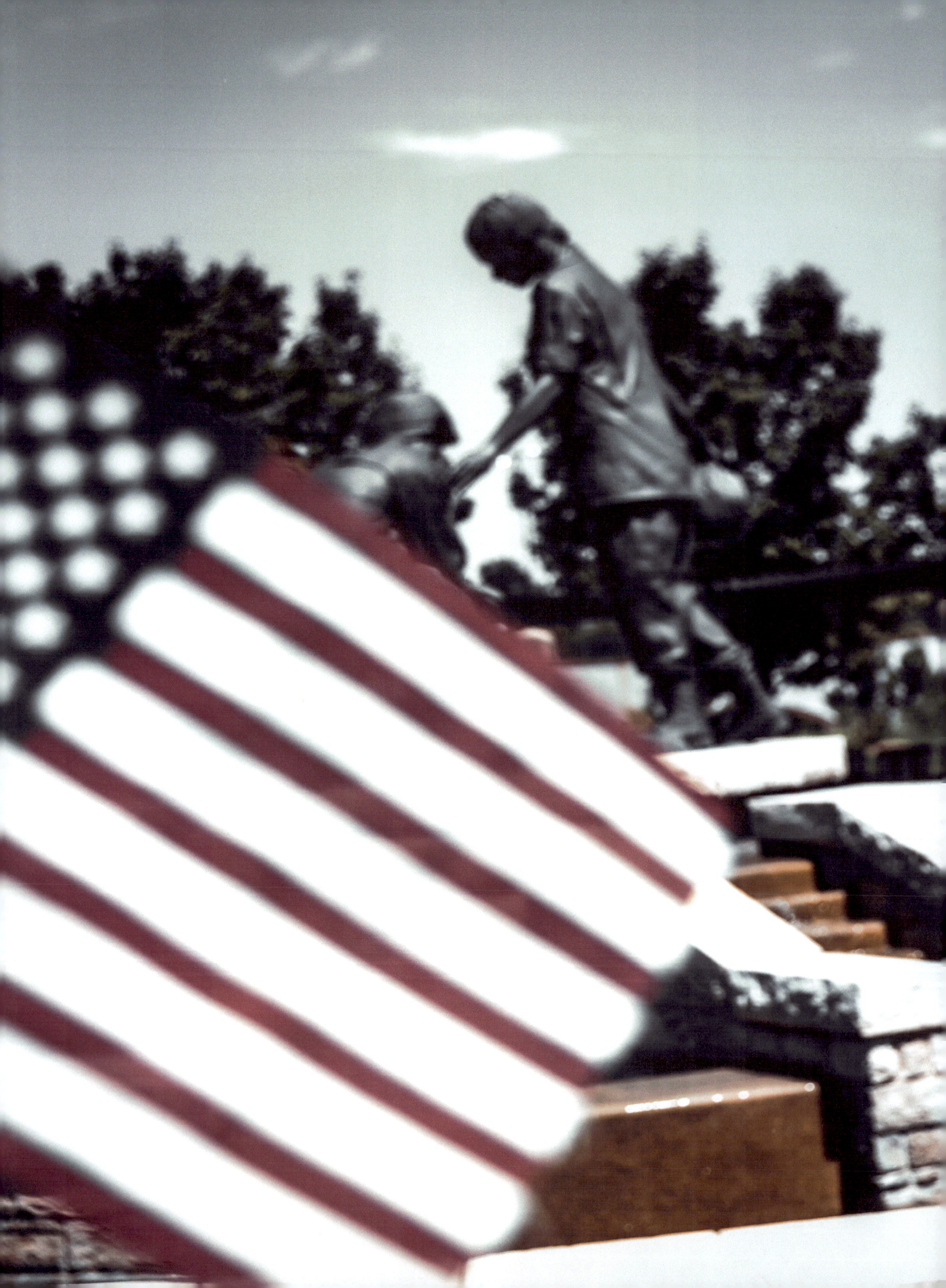

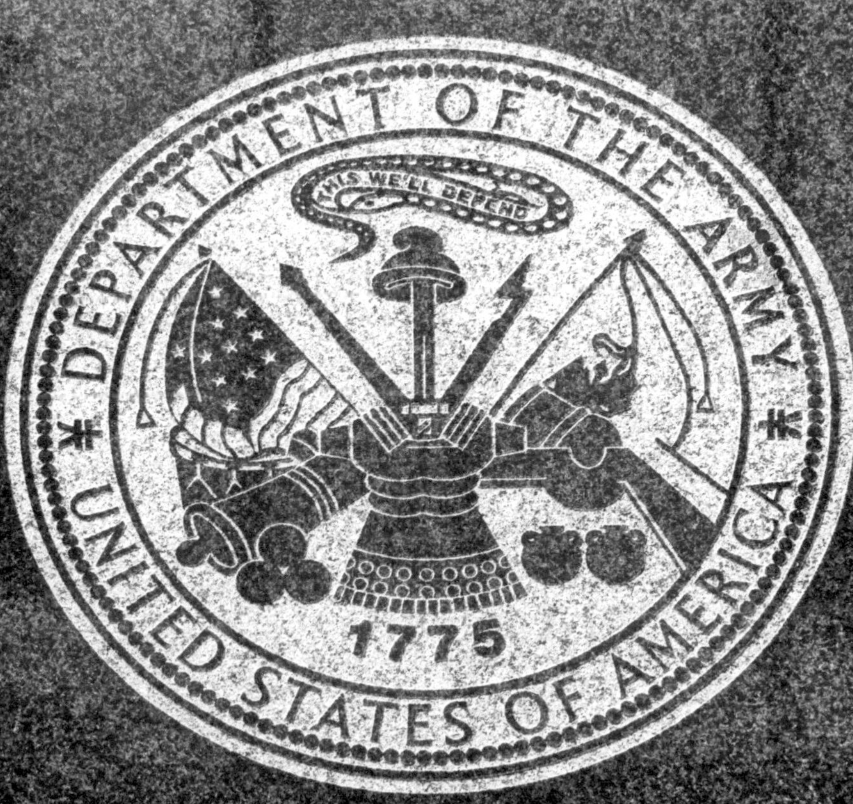

THIS WE'LL DEFEND
DEPARTMENT OF THE ARMY
UNITED STATES OF AMERICA
1775

<u>Dedicated To:</u>

Family & Friends

Armed Forces & Those Whom Have Served for Our Country

Photographers & Artists

<u>All Photographs, Artist Expression, Digital Photographs/Edits, Publication & Copyrights-Reserved to:</u>

Sky Fire Photgraphy L.L.C

Photography Location Taken: 104th Ave, Westminster CO. At the Armed Forces Tribute Garden.

If you like to contribute to the memorial;

<u>Pleae email:</u>mlagurard@cityofwestminster.us & City of Westiminster

Arm Forces Insignia Crest & Sculptures are Trademarked and

all rights reserved to the artist and the Army Forces.

All photography is copyrighted by photographer & Sky Fire Photography LLC.

<u>Note:</u> This book contains copyrighted material.

It is determined this to be "fair use" of the copyrighted material

as referenced and provided for in section 107 of the US Copyright Law.

If you wish to use any copyrighted material from this book

for purposes of your own that go beyond fair use,

you must obtain express permission from the copyright owner.

<u>Email for Business Inquiries:</u>

skyfirephotographyl.l.c@gmail.com

Visit Website at www.skyfirephotography.org

Please Enjoy My Photography!